Animal Hom

Written and photographed by Barrie Watts
Illustrated by Andrew Midgley

Collins *Educational*
An imprint of HarperCollins *Publishers*

I am a mole.

I live in a hole.

We are ants.

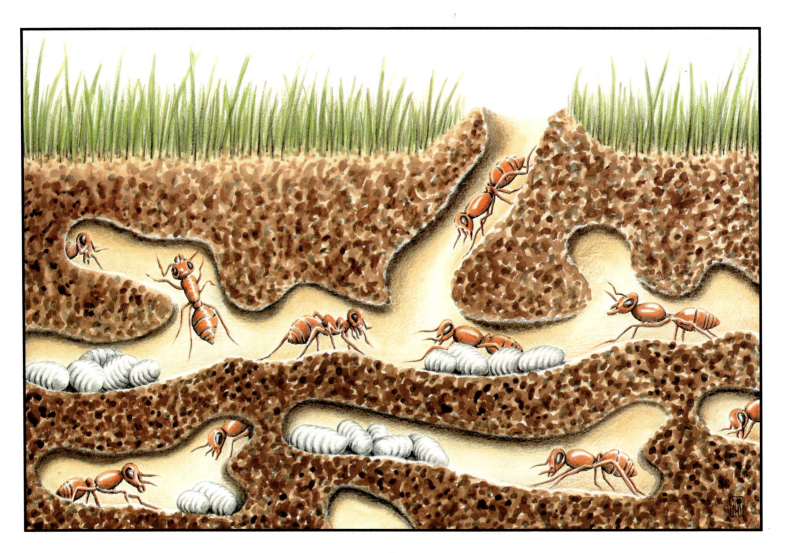

We live underground.

I am a frog.

I live in a pond.

I am a mouse.

I live in a field.

I am a spider.

I live on a web.

We are honeybees.

We live in a hive.

We are blue tits.

We live in a garden.

INDEX

ants 4

blue tit 14

field 9

frog 6

garden 15

hive 13

hole 3

honeybees 12

mole 2

mouse 8

pond 7

spider 10

underground 5

web 11